Touching
the Seasons

NICK FAWCETT

Touching the Seasons

Down-to-earth prayers for the Christian Year

**kevin
mayhew**

First published in 2006 by

KEVIN MAYHEW LTD

Buxhall, Stowmarket, Suffolk, IP14 3BW

E-mail: info@kevinmayhew.com

www.kevinmayhew.com

9 8 7 6 5 4 3 2 1 0

ISBN 1 84417 499 9

Catalogue No. 1500865

Cover design by Sara-Jane Came

Edited and typeset by Katherine Laidler

Printed and bound in Great Britain

Contents

Introduction   9

ADVENT AND CHRISTMAS

 1 The expectant mother   12
 2 The late train   13
 3 The meal table   14
 4 The spent battery   15
 5 The traffic policeman   16
 6 The horoscope   17
 7 The painter   18
 8 The World Cup defeat   19
 9 The tyre and exhaust centre   20
10 The carol singers   21
11 The disobedient child   22
12 The Christmas shopping   23
13 The holly   24
14 The mistletoe   25
15 The Christmas wrapping paper   26
16 The Christmas crackers   27
17 The Christmas tree   28
18 The Christmas meal   29
19 The Christmas present   30
20 The Christmas stocking   31
21 The Christmas cards   32
22 The Christmas cake   33
23 The Advent candle   34
24 The candlelight service   35
25 The Christmas pudding   36
26 The Christmas lights   37
27 The family get-together   38
28 The frost   39

29 The turkey leftovers   40
30 The Advent calendar   41

OLD AND NEW YEAR

31 The discarded diary   44
32 The new calendar   45

EPIPHANY

33 The dawn chorus   48
34 The floodlights   49

MOTHER'S DAY

35 The harassed mother   52

LENT

36 The cream cake   54
37 The one-way street   55
38 The health check   56
39 The comma   57
40 The frown   58
41 The fireplace   59
42 The game of hide-and-seek   60
43 The salt   61
44 The missing slate   62
45 The sandcastle   63
46 The impressionist   64
47 The nun   65
48 The proofreader   66
49 The loose screw   67
50 The moth-eaten clothes   68
51 The vitamin tablets   69
52 The architect's drawings   70
53 The long-distance lorry driver   71
54 The world record attempt   72
55 The paperweight   73

56 The diet   74
57 The second helping   75
58 The child's homework   76
59 The peacock   77
60 The saucepan of milk   78
61 The pornographic photograph   79
62 The skinflint   80
63 The luxury lifestyle   81
64 The volunteer   82
65 The confession   83
66 The phone call   84
67 The lost-property office   85
68 The sergeant-major   86
69 The cost of living   87
70 The crucifix   88
71 The flock of sheep   89

HOLY WEEK

72 The royal visit   92
73 The coins   93
74 The glass of wine   94
75 The by-election defeat   95
76 The pricked finger   96
77 The hot cross buns   97
78 The broken vase   98

EASTER

79 The daffodils   100
80 The Easter eggs   101
81 The tall story   102
82 The bouncy ball   104
83 The coffin   105
84 The newspaper exposé   106
85 The school run   107
86 The rabbits   108

87 The Easter bank holiday   109
88 The solar eclipse   110

ASCENSION DAY

89 The view   112
90 The honours list   113

PENTECOST

91 The wind farm   116
92 The iron smelting   117

TRINITY SUNDAY

93 The 3-D glasses   120
94 The relations   121

FATHER'S DAY

95 The Father's Day card   124

HARVEST THANKSGIVING

96 The good and bad harvests   126
97 The fruit bowl   127

ALL SAINTS' DAY

98 The teacher   130
99 The rare breeds park   131

REMEMBRANCE DAY

100 The war memorial   134

Introduction

Some days of the year are special, aren't they? Not just Christmas and Easter, but other occasions, Christian or otherwise, capture the imagination and call for a response. We feel at such times that our prayers should reflect their significance, but we're not always able to articulate our thoughts as we would wish to or to relate the occasion in question to daily life.

This book seeks to address that problem, offering a hundred simple prayers rooted in everyday experience, the commonplace offering a springboard to personal devotion. Through things as mundane as turkey leftovers, a discarded diary, a fruit bowl or saucepan of milk, prayer is brought down to earth, ordinary items, events, people and experiences time and again suggesting ways in which those special days of the year are touched by God's hand. It is my hope that such things will speak to you as they have spoken to me.

NICK FAWCETT

To Mark and Anne Sheen

with thanks for special times shared.

ADVENT
AND CHRISTMAS

1
The expectant mother

She was counting down the days,
   scarcely able to contain her excitement,
   knowing that when the child came
   life would never be the same again.
Would it be early?
Would it be late?
Who could say.
But the day *would* come, sure enough.

Lord, you tell us to look forward,
   anticipating the dawn of your kingdom.
I've no idea when that shall be
   or what it will mean,
   but, however long the wait,
   teach me to look forward expectantly,
   assured that the day will come:
   a day that will transform not only *my life*,
   but the whole world, for ever.
Amen.

2
The late train

They'd been waiting for hours,
    their frustration growing by the minute;
    yet there was still no sign of the train,
    nor any explanation for the delay . . .
    and eventually a few gave up,
    their patience at an end,
    taking a taxi instead.
And the rest?
You've guessed it.
No sooner had those few gone
    than the train pulled in at the station.

It's hard to keep faith that your kingdom will come, Lord,
    for so much in the world seems to deny your love
    and frustrate your will.
However hard it may be, though,
    help me to trust in your promises,
    daring to believe the day will come,
    despite everything that conspires against it,
    when your love finally triumphs over all.
Amen.

3
The meal table

The table was laid,
    the places set,
    everything ready for the arrival of the guests.
When would they come?
Who could say.
So much depending on the traffic,
    the weather,
    their plans for the day,
    but come they would,
    and when they did so
    all would be ready,
    a welcome assured.

Help me, Lord, in all my preparations for Christmas –
    the writing of cards,
    buying of presents,
    wrapping of gifts,
    decorating the home –
    to make ready for you,
    preparing myself in heart and mind
    to worship you afresh
    and welcome you more fully into my life,
    so that when the day of your coming finally dawns,
    I may be ready to greet you and celebrate a banquet,
    not at *my* table
    but *yours*.
Amen.

4
The spent battery

'Ever Ready', they called it,
    but it wasn't,
    for, like any other battery,
    it soon ran dry,
    completely drained after a few days' service,
    of no use at all.
Yes, it still looked the part,
    enough to fool anyone,
    but when put to the test the truth became clear:
    it was an empty shell,
    devoid of life.

I like to think *I'm* ready, Lord –
    to serve you,
    respond to your call
    and welcome you when you come again –
    but am I actually anywhere near it,
    or has the life that coursed within me drained away,
    energy and enthusiasm dissipated,
    leaving behind a discipleship that flatters to deceive?
Come, Lord, and fill me afresh,
    that I may live and work for you.
Amen.

5
The traffic policeman

He pointed the way,
    shepherding the traffic past the accident
    and back on to the road –
    not a glamorous job
    but an important one nonetheless,
    showing us the way to take
    in order to continue our journey safely.

Help me, Lord, to point to *your* way,
    so that others in turn may find guidance
    in their journey of life.
May all I say, do, think and am
    point away from me
    and towards you.
Amen.

6
The horoscope

Do some actually believe it?
It's hard to credit,
    for could anyone seriously imagine
    their fortunes today
    or fate tomorrow
    are linked to the movement of stars light-years distant,
    and shared by countless others across the world
    with nothing else in common but their date of birth?
Apparently so,
    for why else would the column be printed,
    week in, week out,
    unless the publishers assume
    some people are gullible enough
    to take it seriously?

Remind me, Lord, that you alone truly know the future,
    your promises of old
    having found fulfilment in Christ,
    the message of the Law and prophets
    vindicated by his birth, death and resurrection.
Help me,
    remembering all you have so faithfully done,
    to trust in all you will yet do,
    confident that,
    in the fullness of time,
    your will shall be done
    and your kingdom come.
Amen.

7
The painter

He could have slapped on the paint any old how,
    plastered it over the pitted and peeling surface
    with barely a second thought,
    and for a time, at least, I'd have been none the wiser,
    any defects being hidden from view.
But they'd have shown through eventually,
    the lack of care and preparation bound to surface,
    and before long it would have needed doing again,
    things no better than they were before.

Save me, Lord,
    from carelessness in my relationship with you,
    from being casual and complacent in my dealings,
    assuming I can gloss over
    whatever's wrong between us.
Teach me to work at my faith,
    preparing the ground each day to know you better,
    so that when your kingdom comes
    I may be ready to stand before you
    and meet you, face to face.
Amen.

8
The World Cup defeat

It was the biggest upset for years,
    the rank outsiders defeating the team of stars –
    a sensational result that left the pundits speechless,
    the victors exultant
    and the losers cringing with embarrassment,
    rudely brought back down to earth.
They'd considered themselves the elite,
    the match a mere formality,
    but they'd been humbled,
    humiliated,
    the tables turned
    and the proud brought down from their throne.

Teach me, Lord,
    that you are a God who repeatedly turns the tables,
    the way of Christ, if taken seriously,
    challenging the assumptions of this world
    and upsetting the status quo.
Teach me that, though it may not sometimes seem like it,
    you will finally correct injustice,
    overcome evil
    and undo wrongs,
    in your kingdom the first being last
    and the last first.
Help me, then, to trust in your purpose
    and to walk humbly with you.
Amen.

9

The tyre and exhaust centre

I didn't have time to hang around,
  nor money to waste, come to that,
  so the centre was ideal for my needs,
  allowing me to pop in on the off-chance
  and have both exhaust and tyres replaced,
  the job tackled on the spot,
  problem solved.

When I look at the world, Lord –
  its tensions and suffering,
  need and heartbreak –
  it's hard not to wonder what you're doing
  and why you take so long to put things right,
  for so much within it seems to question your love
  and undermine your will.
Help me to understand, though,
  that there are no quick fixes or short-term solutions,
  but that you are working nonetheless,
  your purpose destined to triumph,
  not in *my* time
  but in *yours*.
Amen.

10
The carol singers

They sang to fill their pockets,
  croaking a desultory verse in the hope of some reward.

They sang to fill their churches,
  hoping that some who listened
  might turn up that Sunday.

They sang to fill empty stomachs,
  their aim to raise money for charity.

There are all kinds of reasons, Lord, for singing carols –
  some good,
  some bad –
  but teach me to sing, above all,
  simply to celebrate your love
  and to share it with others.
May I sing from the heart
  in joyful praise
  and true worship.
Amen.

11

The disobedient child

'Do as you're told!' said the teacher,
   but he wouldn't,
   instead staring at her defiantly,
   resolved to do his own thing,
   come what may.

Forgive me, Lord, for so often *I'm* disobedient,
   ignoring your call and defying your will,
   preferring my way to yours.
Teach me, instead, like Mary long ago,
   to listen to your voice
   and humbly to obey,
   putting your will before my own –
   self second
   and you first.
Amen.

12

The Christmas shopping

There was so much to buy,
 and there were many to buy for,
 the cost of it all mounting by the day,
 enough for me to consider a second mortgage!
I wanted to be generous –
 nothing wrong with that –
 but I went over the top,
 much of what I bought unnecessary –
 neither needed nor wanted.

Forgive me, Lord,
 for I fritter away money on trivialities
 while a world goes hungry,
 this season of goodwill to *all*
 turned into one of good things for *me*.
Teach me to make room in my celebrations
 for those who, in this life, have so little to celebrate
 and to give as generously to them
 as you have given to me.
Amen.

13
The holly

It made a lovely display,
    the redness of the berries
    picked out against the foliage,
    each sprig woven together into a festive garland
    evocative of Yuletide cheer and goodwill.

Only suddenly it spoke differently,
    the berries recalling drops of blood
    and the foliage a crown of thorns,
    the result not so much a garland as a wreath,
    evocative of sorrow and suffering.

Remind me, Lord, that after the stable came a cross,
    after birth, death,
    after celebration, sacrifice,
    and after pleasure, pain,
    each bound by a single stem:
    the wonder of your love.
Help me to rejoice in all that this season means,
    not just in part but in full.
Amen.

14

The mistletoe

It was a bit of fun, that's all –
    a quick kiss under the mistletoe –
    but it caught the spirit of the season:
    a time for breaking down barriers
    and bringing people together;
    of goodwill to all.
But, of course, the kiss meant little –
    a sign of affection, perhaps,
    but the closeness more apparent than real.

You, Lord, speak of a different kind of closeness,
    not just with others but above all with you,
    made possible through your coming among us,
    sharing our humanity
    and dying our death to bring us life.
Help me to celebrate the love at the heart of this season –
    the relationship you offer in Christ –
    and, through him, draw me closer to you each day.
Amen.

15
The Christmas wrapping paper

I'd spent hours choosing it,
    each sheet picked out with a particular person in mind,
    and I'd wrapped the presents with care,
    complete with ribbon and label,
    every one of them a labour of love.
Yet it was wasted, of course,
    the parcels torn open in haste
    with barely a look at what covered them –
    the gift inside all that counted.

Though much of the packaging surrounding Christmas
    needs discarding, Lord –
    having nothing to do with its true meaning –
    save me from overlooking
    the love and care you showed
    in preparing the way of Christ.
Help me, if I would fully celebrate your gift,
    to appreciate the context in which you gave it –
    the history of your people,
    teaching of the Law
    and message of the prophets,
    each finding glorious fulfilment
    in the Word made flesh.
For your Son
    and all that points to him and your love,
    thank you!
Amen.

16

The Christmas crackers

They promised much,
  each holding out the prospect of delights within,
  but it was all show,
  the contents disappointing to say the least:
  a flimsy hat,
  feeble joke
  and worthless gift.

For so many, Lord,
  despite the glitz, bustle, hype and expense,
  it's not just crackers but Christmas itself
  that proves to be a let-down,
  promising much yet delivering little.
Awaken the hearts of all
  to the glorious surprise at its heart –
  the wonder of your Son,
  born in a stable and laid in a manger,
  your Word made flesh and love incarnate –
  a gift beyond price that will never disappoint.
Amen.

17

The Christmas tree

It looked drab when we bought it,
  the branches curiously stark,
  but when we added the tinsel, pine cones,
  baubles and lights,
  suddenly it was transformed into something magical,
  irresistibly drawing the eye.

Teach me, Lord, to put *you* at the centre of Christmas,
  so that it may not just be a *tree* that's transformed
  but *me* –
  the things I do,
  the way I think,
  the person I am,
  each touched by your presence
  and made new by your love.
Amen.

18
The Christmas meal

It took ages to prepare,
    countless hours of peeling, washing,
    cooking and fretting,
    never mind the time spent buying everything in
    and the washing-up afterwards –
    hour upon hour for a single meal.
I enjoyed it, of course,
    don't get me wrong,
    for it was a feast fit for a king,
    and, yes, an expected part of Christmas,
    but I couldn't help feeling uneasy,
    wondering whether all that time
    couldn't have been better spent.

How much time, Lord,
    will I make for *you* this Christmas?
How much time,
    before, during and after the celebrations,
    to reflect on your love?
Will I be able to measure it in hours, days,
    or will it be just brief snatches,
    a moment here and there
    included almost as an afterthought?
Forgive me,
    for all too often,
    at Christmas or otherwise,
    I have time for just about everything . . .
    except you.
Amen.

19
The Christmas present

Was my effort appreciated?
Probably not.
The hours of thinking what to buy,
   shopping around
   and then lovingly wrapping it,
   scarcely even considered.
But that didn't matter,
   for I wasn't looking for thanks,
   my sole motive in buying the gift
   being to bring pleasure –
   to add to my child's happiness and express my love.

Thank you, Lord, for *your* love,
   constantly reaching out
   though I fail to appreciate all you've given
   or how much it cost you.
Thank you that your love and goodness
   is not dependent on my deserving,
   but goes on being poured out day after day,
   generous beyond measure.
Amen.

20
The Christmas stocking

I'll never forget that look on their faces
    as they hung their stockings –
    the excitement and sense of wonder
    that lit up their eyes
    as they said goodnight and went to bed.
They'd learn soon enough that it was all a charade,
    innocence such as theirs sadly short-lived,
    but while it lasted it held a kind of magic,
    their childlike trust and hope
    speaking of a faith I yearn to share.

Loving Lord, keep alive in me the hopefulness of youth,
    that same sense of joy in simple things
    and expectation for the future.
Though life dishes out knocks and disappointments,
    help me to carry on believing
    in what *you* hold in store –
    no charade, but wonderful beyond words.
Amen.

21
The Christmas cards

I checked the list,
   ticking off the names one by one,
   in most cases this the one time of year I made contact –
   the annual Christmas card
   more a reminder of old friends
   than of enduring relationships;
   a way of telling people they were still remembered,
   still recalled with affection.
I'll be in touch, I said,
   will write again soon,
   and I meant it at the time,
   but the promise, like the people,
   was soon forgotten once more.

For so many, Lord,
   Christmas stirs a sense of your presence,
   reminding them of a reality beyond this world,
   a relationship they crave,
   and for a few days churches bulge at the seams
   as carols are sung
   and the gospel message given a hearing . . .
   but then January sales beckon,
   calling folk back to their true devotion,
   and you are forgotten again for another year.
Break through the trappings of this season
   and touch human hearts the world over,
   so that instead of being briefly remembered,
   you may be known and loved, this and every day.
Amen.

22

The Christmas cake

She made it year after year,
    taking a quiet pride in her achievement
    as she weighed out the ingredients,
    mixed them together,
    baked the cake
    and carefully iced it –
    each step a labour of love.
It was a well-worn ritual,
    but still she brooded and fretted over getting it right,
    concerned it might fail to measure up
    to previous years' standards.

Do I give similar thought, Lord,
    at this or any time of the year,
    to what comprises my *life*,
    carefully weighing the ingredients in the balance
    to ensure I've got them right?
Or have I become casual,
    complacent,
    settling for whatever's on offer,
    without a second thought?
Whatever else I do this season,
    teach me to make room
    for the things that really matter;
    room, above all, for you.
Amen.

23

The Advent candle

It was nearly spent now,
 the candle reduced to a mere stub,
 each time it was lit shortened its life
 until finally it would be no more.

Teach me, Lord, that your coming into the world
 was not without cost;
 that you gave of yourself,
 surrendering your life to bring us light.
Help me, as I celebrate your birth,
 to remember also your death
 and to be ready in turn to give as well as receive
 in the service of your kingdom.
Amen.

24
The candlelight service

It was a lovely occasion –
   unforgettable,
   the candles shining like stars in the darkness,
   the choir serenading us like angels,
   and the carols, prayers and readings
   conjuring up images of Christmas past,
   cosy and reassuring –
   such that I went on my way with a warm glow,
   feeling that the season had truly started,
   full of festive cheer.

Forgive me, Lord,
   for though my worship was well intended,
   it was finally more about *me* than you –
   about *my* enjoyment,
   my feelings,
   my idea of what Christmas should be all about –
   familiarity immunising me
   to the true wonder of your love.
Help me to see beyond the trappings and traditions
   of this season
   to the awesome truth they proclaim:
   your Word,
   your Son,
   your love,
   your gift,
   Good News, now and always.
Amen.

25
The Christmas pudding

It was a luxury pudding,
   laced with brandy,
   stuffed with fruit and nuts;
   but another pudding at another time
   would have yielded something extra:
   a silver coin or some such concealed within –
   for the finder a bonus indeed.

Teach me, Lord,
   amid the festivity and merriment of this season,
   to delve deeper,
   discovering what's of real value within it:
   the new life you offer through your Son,
   bringing nourishment to body, mind and soul.
Help me to find for myself that most precious gift of all.
Amen.

26
The Christmas lights

It was a pleasing spectacle,
    the display bringing some welcome sparkle
    to the drab days of winter,
    dispelling the darkness and lifting the spirit.
But they were soon gone,
    taken down once Christmas was over
    and packed away for another year.

Open my heart, Lord, to the radiance of your love,
    the light that shone in the birth of your Son
    and that continues to shine today,
    nothing able to overcome it.
Help me to glimpse afresh
    the true romance of this season,
    the full wonder and beauty of it all,
    able to shed light in my heart not just at Christmas
    but each moment of every day.
Amen.

27
The family get-together

It's a special time,
  bringing families together across the world –
  parents with children,
  brothers with sisters,
  grandparents with grandchildren,
  aunts and uncles with nieces and nephews –
  this is a season for reunions,
  for drawing close once more.

Remind me, Lord,
  that Christmas speaks of another family,
  embracing all the world –
  the family of your children,
  united in your love.
May Christmas truly be a time of coming together;
  a time when,
  remembering the One made flesh,
  we learn to celebrate and honour
  our common humanity,
  barriers broken and divisions overcome.
Amen.

28
The frost

It lay thick on the ground,
    holding the world in its icy grip –
    soil rock hard,
    leaves scorched,
    buds nipped,
    water turned to ice –
    yet already new growth was stirring,
    bulbs swelling,
    snowdrops lifting their dainty heads,
    and winter shrubs blossoming in joyful defiance.

Remind me, Lord,
    that even in the darkest days of life
    and the bleak chill of death,
    you are there,
    bringing new beginnings.
For your life-giving power,
    beyond containment,
    receive my praise.
Amen.

29
The turkey leftovers

It was *turkey* again,
    as it had been each day that week –
    cold for supper,
    in sandwiches for tea,
    in soup for lunch –
    the same ingredient, it seemed, for every meal
    as the carcass was stripped to the bone.
We'd eaten it at first with relish,
    but now there was almost a sigh,
    a groan of 'Not again!' as it was served up once more.

I grow tired of *most* things eventually, Lord,
    even those that are special;
    what I greeted once with joy and gratitude
    now viewed with disdain.
Forgive my over-familiarity with the wonder of your love
    and help me still to celebrate the good news of Christ –
    something to go on getting excited about,
    day after day.
Amen.

30
The Advent calendar

It lay discarded,
   the last window having been opened days since,
   and somehow it summed up the mood of anticlimax –
   Christmas, after weeks of looking forward,
   over and done with for another year.

Though I speak of your coming again, Lord,
   your return to establish your kingdom,
   it's hard to anticipate it meaningfully,
   and part of me doesn't want to,
   for you've given so much here and now that's good,
   and it would seem wrong to overlook this life
   through dwelling on the next.
Yet don't let me lose altogether my sense of expectation;
   that conviction that one day your will shall be done –
   sorrow overcome,
   evils righted,
   love triumphant,
   death itself destroyed.
Help me to celebrate today in the light of your tomorrow.
Amen.

OLD AND NEW YEAR

31

The discarded diary

It was strange, thumbing through it,
    for scribbled notes that had spoken of the future
    spoke now of the past,
    and occasions once keenly anticipated
    were now barely remembered,
    each part of my past instead of my future,
    over and done with, for better or worse.

Thank you, Lord, that in pleasure and pain,
    triumph and tragedy,
    hope and fear,
    health and sickness,
    you've been with me across another year,
    leading me safely through its ups and downs,
    highs and lows.
Teach me, recalling your faithful guidance,
    to trust you for all that lies ahead,
    knowing that you alone will be the same,
    yesterday, today and tomorrow.
Amen.

32

The new calendar

It still feels special, even now.
After all my years of life,
    with their rollercoaster of joy and sorrow,
    there's still something magical about a new page,
    new month,
    new year,
    waiting to unfold its secrets.

I'm not so naive, Lord,
    as to think everything will work out as I hope,
    offering untarnished joy and unbroken fulfilment,
    for I know well enough life isn't like that,
    being just as likely to bring tears as laughter,
    and dismay as delight,
    but teach me, whatever the days ahead may bring,
    to remember that you will be there by my side,
    able to lead me from the old to the new,
    and in all things working together for good.
Amen.

EPIPHANY

33

The dawn chorus

It was a wonderful sound:
    a chorus of birdsong filling the still morning air,
    exultant and ecstatic;
    a jubilant psalm of praise to welcome the rising sun,
    celebrating a new day after the long hours of darkness.

Thank you, Lord, for the new day you bring
    through the rising of your *Son*,
    the new beginnings,
    new life,
    you daily make possible through him.
Thank you for your promise that,
    however deep the darkness may seem,
    light will dawn again,
    shining in our hearts for evermore.
Amen.

34
The floodlights

The night was drawing in,
   darkness descending,
   but it made no difference to the game,
   for the floodlights were on,
   illuminating the ground,
   allowing the fans to see every pass,
   every dribble,
   every shot,
   every goal.

Thank you, Lord, for *your* light,
   guiding to Bethlehem,
   shining on the mountain,
   pouring from the empty tomb
   and sparkling in our hearts.
Thank you for the knowledge that,
   whatever life brings,
   you will give light to my path,
   this and every day.
Amen.

MOTHER'S DAY

35

The harassed mother

She struggled with the screaming child,
   juggling the shopping with one hand,
   the pushchair with the other,
   striving to offer comfort as best she could,
   but all too conscious of the countless tasks still to do,
   the duties of another day yet to be completed.
And I realised suddenly
   how easily we take mothers for granted,
   forgetting the love that brought us into being,
   that nurtured and sustained us,
   comforting, encouraging, teaching and protecting,
   day after day,
   year after year.

I take *you* for granted, Lord,
   forgetting the way you hold me in your arms,
   as a mother cradles her child;
   the way you teach, provide, comfort and lead,
   always there when I need you most.
Help me to respond,
   not just today but every day,
   in grateful and loving service.
Amen.

LENT

36

The cream cake

'Naughty but nice', they called it,
   and they were right,
   for though it wasn't the best thing for my health,
   it was delicious nonetheless,
   every mouthful a delight –
   enough for me to have another,
   the next day . . .
   and the next . . .
   and the next.

Some things, Lord, are indeed innocent enough,
   genuinely 'naughty but nice',
   but others are different,
   the dangers they bring greater than I realise
   and any pleasure less fulfilling than might first appear,
   either bringing happiness that doesn't last
   or won at a cost to others,
   causing them hurt and sorrow.
Teach me, then, when temptation comes,
   to look beneath the surface,
   and beyond myself,
   and to consider where yielding might lead.
Amen.

37

The one-way street

I wanted to turn around and take another route
    but I couldn't,
    the one-way system forcing me to carry on,
    whether I liked it or not,
    until I reached the end.

I remember, Lord,
    how Jesus had to choose in the wilderness
    between the way of self or others –
    and how he chose the latter,
    knowing it would mean suffering and sacrifice,
    the agony of death on a cross,
    and knowing too that once he started out
    there could be no turning back.
Help me to follow you with similar commitment,
    ready to walk your way to my journey's end.
Amen.

38
The health check

It was a thorough examination,
    a check on just about everything you could think of,
    and a good thing too,
    for it showed up problems
    he hadn't begun to notice,
    nipping them in the bud
    before they could cause serious harm.
A few months' delay,
    or a less careful doctor,
    and who can say what would have happened,
    whether he'd even be here now to tell the tale?

Examine me, Lord,
    and know my thoughts.
Search me,
    and help me to see where I'm spiritually weak,
    my faith lacking
    and my commitment poor.
Put a new heart and a right spirit within me,
    and, by your grace, make me whole.
Amen.

39

The comma

Who'd have thought it –
   something as small as a comma
   making such a difference?
But it did,
   the sentence making little sense without it.
It indicated a pause for breath,
   small but vital;
   that little break key to the whole.

Remind me, Lord, that *I* need to pause sometimes
   if I'm to make sense of life;
   time to stop and stare essential
   if I'm to keep things in balance
   and live as you intend.
In the many demands and duties I face each day,
   teach me to make space for stillness and quiet –
   space for me and you.
Amen.

40
The frown

It made me uneasy, that look on his face,
  feeling that I'd done something wrong,
  somehow displeased him.
But I'd misunderstood entirely,
  his frown one of concentration rather than anger,
  and my discomfort in his presence
  altogether misplaced.

Too easily, Lord,
  and at this season in particular,
  I picture you with a frown on your face –
  stern,
  forbidding,
  angry –
  as though you are permanently displeased
  at my behaviour,
  looking for the opportunity to step in and condemn.
Remind me that the reality is so very different,
  your nature always to have mercy,
  to forgive, love and accept.
Help me, then,
  during Lent and always,
  to celebrate your love that smiles upon me.
Amen.

41
The fireplace

I raked out the ashes,
  intending to discard them
  and light the fire from scratch,
  but then I stopped in surprise,
  for a few embers were faintly glowing,
  well spent yet still alight,
  sufficient to be fanned back into life –
  a little kindling here,
  a few coals there,
  and flames rose anew –
  the fire once more ablaze.

Too often, Lord, the flame of my faith dies down,
  the commitment that once burned so brightly
  now barely smouldering,
  lofty intentions turned to ashes
  and ardour all but cold.
Yet from the dying embers
  you bring new life,
  rekindling the fire of faith.
Come now
  and reignite my love,
  so that it may burn afresh for you.
Amen.

42
The game of hide-and-seek

It was an excellent hiding place,
    the last spot anyone would think to look,
    and for a moment the child was flummoxed,
    unsure where to turn next.
But he refused to give up,
    continuing instead with his search
    until it was at last rewarded –
    the problem solved,
    truth revealed.

Teach me, Lord, that your call to seek and find
    is not a one-off instruction –
    advice we can act on once and then forget about –
    but an indispensable guideline for discipleship,
    to be persevered with throughout the journey of faith.
Help me, then,
    to search patiently for greater understanding,
    deeper commitment
    and a fuller love for you and others,
    assured that if I truly seek such things,
    I *will* find.
Amen.

43
The salt

It made such a difference,
   turning a bland serving into a delicious meal
   full of flavour,
   a joy to taste.

Help *me* to make a difference, Lord –
   if not to be salt of the earth,
   then at least to change something,
   somewhere,
   for the better.
Help me,
   through serving others,
   to serve you.
 Amen.

44

The missing slate

There was one missing, that's all,
    a single slate absent in an otherwise perfect roof,
    and it seemed so minor a fault that I brushed it aside –
    too trivial a problem to trifle with.
But when the rain came in
    and the ceiling collapsed,
    I learned the hard way that even one thing missing,
    however small,
    can be one too many,
    its effects out of all proportion to its size.

Teach me, Lord, that,
    however strong my faith or deep my commitment,
    if love is missing, then the rest is flawed
    and all the devotion and piety in the world
    can never redress the balance.
Whatever else I lack, then,
    may your love flow within me –
    the ground and goal of all my being.
Amen.

45
The sandcastle

We built it together,
   piling up bucket-loads of sand,
   building turrets,
   constructing walls,
   shoring up the defences . . .
   but then stood back to watch it fall,
   the tide creeping inexorably closer –
   nibbling at the edges,
   swirling round the base,
   and then finally sweeping it away altogether,
   as though it had never been.

My life, Lord, is like that,
   the happiness I find and goals I strive for
   like castles on the beach,
   destined to be destroyed;
   so much in this world shifting or easily undermined,
   here today and gone tomorrow.
Teach me to build wisely,
   seeking fulfilment in your love, which, alone,
   is able to face the restless tide
   and still stand firm
   for ever.
Amen.

46
The impressionist

He had the voices off to a tee,
   the expressions and mannerisms as well,
   his routine bringing to life,
   in rapid-fire succession,
   a host of celebrities –
   politicians, sports stars, actors and royalty –
   almost as though they were there in person
   rather than an imitation of the real thing.

What impression do I give to others, Lord –
   above all, what impression of *you*?
You call me to imitate Christ,
   reflecting something of his light and love;
   do I get anywhere close to that,
   or is my discipleship a caricature of what it should be,
   grotesquely wide of the mark?
Though I will always fall short,
   help me, I pray, to be a little more like Jesus,
   my life in some way speaking to others of him.
Amen.

47

The nun

She'd renounced the world and denied herself,
    committing her life totally to God
    and the cause of his kingdom.
It seemed a drastic step to me,
    one I would never even consider,
    but she was unquestionably sincere,
    her faith making a difference to her life
    in a way mine barely begins to.

Lord, I talk too glibly of sacrifice and self-denial,
    when in reality I live almost wholly for my own ends,
    unwilling to surrender even a little for you or others,
    and through my failure to deny myself
    I daily deny you.
Give me a genuine commitment to Christ
    that shows itself in action;
    a faith that makes a difference to who and what I am,
    unmistakable to all.
Amen.

48
The proofreader

She examined the proofs,
   poring over each page line by line,
   word by word,
   painstakingly searching for any errors
   that might detract from the finished book.

Examine me, Lord,
   and show me what's wrong in my life.
Search me
   and help me to recognise where I go astray.
Teach me to look carefully at who and what I am,
   identifying my faults and weaknesses,
   and, with your help, seeking to put them right,
   so that, imperfect as I am,
   I may nonetheless draw a little closer
   to what I'm meant to be
   and what I hunger to become.
Amen.

49

The loose screw

It wasn't a problem at first,
    everything continuing to work much as it should,
    but gradually the screw worked looser,
    until it finally fell out altogether,
    with catastrophic results.
Had I tightened it sooner,
    taking just a few moments to put things right,
    I'd have saved such hassle,
    but I underestimated the problem
    and paid the price.

Help me to see, Lord, where my relationship with you
    is not as it should be,
    not as secure or as close as I like to think.
However trivial my faults may seem,
    save me from taking them too lightly –
    from putting off tackling them so long
    that things slip once too often
    and I fall completely from your side.
Amen.

50
The moth-eaten clothes

It was a posh do,
    none of your casual clothes for this one,
    so I went to the wardrobe to pick out my best outfit . . .
    only to gasp in dismay
    for it was best no longer,
    moths having enjoyed a feast,
    leaving the suit in tatters.

Remind me, Lord, that nothing in life lasts for ever,
    the world's beauty, joy and pleasure,
    special though they are,
    being all too fleeting,
    ours but for a moment.
Help me, then, to celebrate such gifts,
    but never to pin my happiness upon them,
    seeking rather treasure in heaven,
    your kingdom that will neither fade nor perish.
Amen.

51
The vitamin tablets

Did I need them?
Probably not,
    but I took them anyway,
    better safe than sorry.
I ate well enough, truth be told,
    but why leave anything to chance?
For, after all,
    few things matter more than health.

Teach me, Lord, how lucky I am
    compared to millions across the world;
    so many having barely enough to survive,
    let alone the good things I take for granted.
Teach me to focus on their *needs* rather than my *extras*
    and to realise that through giving a little
    I can bring them *much*.
Amen.

52
The architect's drawings

They gave a picture of what might be,
    a sense of how something old and dilapidated
    could be transformed,
    new life breathed into it,
    potential hidden for so long at last unlocked.
It would take time, of course,
    effort too,
    but if the will was there,
    then the goal could be reached,
    the dream realised.

You offer in Christ, Lord, a picture of what *life* can be,
    what *I* can be –
    everything made new –
    yet I struggle to believe it possible,
    for I fall so far short
    and find it hard to change even a little.
Teach me that,
    provided I'm serious about commitment
    and prepared to play my part,
    you can do what *I* can't –
    fashion a new creation
    from the unpromising material of my life.
Amen.

53
The long-distance lorry driver

He'd driven for miles,
   hour upon hour on the motorway,
   but his journey wasn't over,
   not by a long way.
There was still a distance to go,
   and he'd be travelling again the next day . . .
   and the next . . .
   the bulk of his life spent on the road.

Remind me, Lord,
   that the journey of discipleship isn't over,
   however far I may have come;
   that each day brings new roads and horizons
   to explore,
   so much still lying before me.
Save me in this life from ever thinking I've arrived,
   but, instead, keep me travelling with you,
   until the pilgrimage is over
   and I enter your kingdom at last.
Amen.

54
The world record attempt

It was a tall order,
    the world record having stood for years,
    but they were resolved to beat it,
    to run their hearts out in a bid for glory.
And try they did,
    pushing themselves to the very last,
    until they collapsed breathless over the finishing line,
    a hair's breadth short of their dream.

Teach me, Lord, to use this season to set new targets,
    more ambitious goals;
    resolved to know, love and serve you better.
Though I've failed before and will fail again,
    instead of being content merely to plod along
    may I truly strive to grow in grace.
Amen.

55
The paperweight

I wouldn't have been able to work without it,
    or at least not outside in the garden,
    for even a gentle breeze was enough to catch the pages
    and send them fluttering across the lawn,
    the carefully arranged sheets scattered in an instant,
    strewn in the mud and flower-beds.
The paperweight, though, solved the problem,
    holding every page secure.

May your love, Lord, keep hold of me
    in the daily round of life.
Though I'm buffeted by temptation
    and exposed to the wind of change,
    save me from being tossed about
    by the restless current.
Secure me through your love
    so that I shall not go astray.
Amen.

56
The diet

He was determined to lose weight,
    suddenly aware of his spreading girth
    and sagging stomach,
    so he cut out those little extras
    that he'd come to take for granted –
    a packet of crisps and pint of beer,
    bar of chocolate and takeaway meal,
    everything in fact that compounded the problem –
    for the first time in his life putting health first,
    pleasure second.

Help me to give something up for Lent, Lord,
    not because it's expected or out of empty show
    but to promote my spiritual health.
Enable me, with your help,
    to cut out whatever undermines my discipleship,
    denying your love and frustrating your purpose;
    whatever, in other words, creates a barrier between us,
    preventing me from knowing you
    as I should and could.
Amen.

57
The second helping

I didn't need any more,
    for I was full already,
    stuffed to the point of bursting,
    but I couldn't resist another helping
    for it was delicious,
    too good to turn down.
I regretted it later, mind –
    cursed myself for a fool,
    for instead of being pleasurably content,
    I felt bloated,
    uncomfortable, to say the least.

I don't think of myself as a glutton, Lord,
    but I *am*, sometimes,
    eating far more than I need
    while others go hungry.
Help me to recognise when enough is enough,
    and instead of overfeeding myself
    teach me to think of those not fed at all.
Amen.

58
The child's homework

He knew he had to do it
   but he kept on putting it off,
   postponing the evil moment.
And finally, when he could delay it no longer,
   he raced to get it finished –
   the attempt desultory,
   as little as he could get away with.

Forgive me, Lord, for I'm careless in *discipleship*,
   reluctant to move away from the comfort zone.
Forgive the complacency of my commitment,
   my doing as little rather than as much as possible,
   and teach me to offer instead not what I *must*
   but what I *may* do in your service,
   in glad and joyful response.
Amen.

59
The peacock

He paraded his feathers,
    strutting this way and that to attract an audience,
    but though the crowds stopped to marvel,
    potential mates kept their distance,
    seemingly unimpressed by his gaudy display.
Impressive he may have been,
    but, apparently, not impressive enough.

Am *I* proud, Lord?
I try not to be,
    but just occasionally I preen myself in public –
    smug about some achievement
    or self-satisfied about a virtuous deed –
    and there are times when, subconsciously,
    despite my best intentions
    I disparage others,
    assuming my way, understanding or motives
    are better than theirs.
Forgive me
    and help me to follow the pattern of Christ,
    remembering that he, though greater than all,
    counted himself as nothing,
    emptying himself to the point of death
    in order to raise me to life.
Teach me, then, to count others better than myself,
    looking to their interests before my own.
Amen.

60
The saucepan of milk

I left it simmering on the stove,
    gently steaming as it warmed through,
    but I left it too long –
    forgetting the inevitable consequences –
    and the milk boiled over,
    spilling on to the ring below,
    the whole pan wasted.

I know, Lord,
    that I *should* simmer about some things in life –
    injustice, exploitation,
    greed, hatred and violence –
    yet I know also how easily
    anger can spill over into rage,
    destroying and wounding,
    adding to rather than alleviating the world's misery.
Show me when it's right to be angry,
    but help me always to channel it,
    so that it will be a tool for good instead of evil.
Amen.

61
The pornographic photograph

Was it wrong to be attracted by the photo,
   even aroused?
It wasn't and yet it was,
   for, on the one hand, the response was instinctive,
   dictated by a primal urge;
   yet, on the other, it was degrading and demeaning,
   not just to the woman pictured
   but to me and to all –
   as though we can be reduced to objects
   rather than people,
   driven more by lust than love,
   desire than devotion.

Help me, Lord,
   to respect your gifts and treat them wisely,
   conscious that they may be a blessing or a curse,
   a treasure or a toxin.
Help me to celebrate all you have given,
   but to use rather than abuse it.
Amen.

62
The skinflint

He wasn't short of a few bob,
   not by a long way,
   probably taking home
   what the rest of us earned together,
   but when it came to a whip-round
   or buying in the drinks,
   his hand was the last to reach for his pocket,
   his wallet staying firmly shut.

I'm not as mean as him, Lord,
   or at least I hope I'm not,
   but I'm not as generous as I could be either,
   money more important to me than it should be,
   and more of a driving force in my life
   than I like to think.
Teach me to steward it wisely,
   but equally to give it freely,
   lest what I possess ends up possessing me.
Amen.

63
The luxury lifestyle

I envied his way of life,
   for it seemed so carefree and glamorous,
   so full of pleasure –
   just about anything he could ever want
   seemingly his for the asking –
   but the irony was that *he* envied *me*,
   coveting the straightforwardness of my life,
   so far removed
   from the demands and pressures he daily faced.

Forgive me, Lord, for I spend so long yearning
   for what I haven't got
   instead of celebrating what I have.
Teach me to appreciate my many blessings
   and not to begrudge others theirs.
Amen.

64

The volunteer

'Any volunteers?' he asked,
   and immediately we looked away,
   as one in our attempt to avoid his eye
   for we'd plenty to do already,
   none of us relishing the prospect of yet more work
   or added responsibility.
'Let someone else do it,' we thought;
   'someone else share the load –
   not me.'

Am I doing enough, Lord –
   as much as I imagine –
   or am I simply making excuses,
   putting off what I'd rather not face?
Help me truly to serve you,
   not doing as little as I can get away with
   but going the extra mile,
   giving and giving again
   to you who gave your all for me.
Amen.

65
The confession

I could see that he was worried,
    troubled by something deep inside,
    but I couldn't work out what,
    being forced instead to stand by helplessly
    as he wrestled with his demons.
But then, finally, he plucked up courage
    and blurted it out,
    confessing to his little 'crime' –
    small in *my* eyes
    but huge in his.
There were tears then,
    first of sorrow
    but then relief,
    as he realised it was dealt with,
    finished
    and forgiven.

Teach me, Lord, to confess my sins to you
    instead of struggling with guilt
    or hiding away in fear;
    to let go of the burden,
    knowing that you seek to pardon
    rather than condemn,
    bless instead of punish.
Help me, then,
    openly and honestly to acknowledge my faults,
    so that I may find the freedom you alone can give.
Amen.

66
The phone call

She put me on hold with the usual platitudes –
    'Won't be a moment' . . .
    'Your call will be dealt with' . . .
    'Thank you for waiting' –
    and half an hour later I was *still* waiting,
    still listening to the infuriating jingle
    and occasional recorded message,
    apparently forgotten in the queue.

Forgive me, Lord,
    for, time after time, I put *you* on hold,
    making time for you when it suits me
    but then turning to other things,
    forgetting you are even there.
Whatever I'm doing,
    wherever I am,
    help me stay connected –
    ready to listen to your voice
    and respond.
Amen.

67
The lost-property office

It was amazing, the items stored there –
  wallets,
  clothes,
  umbrellas,
  handbags,
  all kinds of things people had left behind –
  some, no doubt, overlooked for a moment,
  others forgotten altogether,
  but each, it would seem, finally given up as lost,
  or at least not considered worth reclaiming.

Forgive me, Lord, for too easily I forget *you*,
  repeatedly overlooking your presence,
  and failing, sometimes for days on end,
  even to give you a second thought.
Teach me what matters most in life –
  your love,
  your will,
  your grace,
  your goodness –
  and whatever else I may forget,
  may I remember *you*.
Amen.

68

The sergeant-major

He bellowed out orders,
   his bark terrifying,
   striking dread into the hearts of the new recruits,
   but it did the trick:
   swiftly turning a disorganised rabble into a crack unit,
   discipline so ingrained
   that each knew their responsibilities back to front
   and could be relied on to fulfil them
   to the smallest detail.

Thank you, Lord, that yours is a gentler way:
   not barking out commands or imposing an iron rule,
   but inviting a response,
   calling me to serve of my own free will.
Yet, though you do not force me to obey,
   give me the discipline I need –
   self-discipline –
   to hear your voice and respond,
   honouring your will
   and playing my part in the work of your kingdom.
Help me to fulfil *my* responsibilities to you
   as faithfully as I can.
Amen.

69
The cost of living

The cost of living, they called it,
    as though everything in this world
    can be brought down to money,
    numbers,
    statistics,
    individual happiness depending on economic success
    and material prosperity.
I know what they mean, of course,
    and they're right in part,
    a life of abject poverty no life at all.
But I know also that true fulfilment
    involves so much more,
    the spirit needing nurture as much as the body.

Remind me, Lord, of the true cost of living,
    and your willingness, through your Son, to pay it.
Help me to receive and celebrate
    the life made possible through him –
    life in all its fullness –
    and to give something back in return
    to you who gave so much.
Amen.

70
The crucifix

He wore it unthinkingly,
  not to symbolise any faith or commitment,
  but as a trinket,
  a fashion accessory,
  nothing more –
  the idea of it having deeper meaning
  never even occurring to him,
  let alone being explored.

Speak afresh, Lord,
  to me and your world,
  of Christ
  and all he continues to mean;
  of the One who carried his cross in a different way,
  staggering under its weight
  until finally *it* carried *him*,
  writhing in agony as the life ebbed away.
However familiar the cross may be,
  save me from taking it for granted
  and forgetting the awesome love of which it speaks.
Amen.

71
The flock of sheep

It took just a single sheep to move,
   and before I knew it they all copied,
   each bleating to the others to follow.
Never mind where they were going
   or what dangers it might bring:
   if it was good enough for one
   it was good enough for the rest.

You won't catch *me* following the crowd –
   that's what I tell myself, Lord –
   but I'm wrong, aren't I,
   the pressure to conform
   or desire to keep up
   sometimes hard to resist.
Despite my best intentions, I go astray, time after time.
Forgive me,
   and teach me to follow not the sheep
   but the shepherd.
Amen.

HOLY WEEK

72

The royal visit

They lined the streets in their thousands,
   cramming into every available space,
   pushing, shoving, and straining their necks
   to get a sight of the royal procession.
No more than that –
   just a fleeting glimpse –
   but it was enough to send them home happy,
   buzzing with excitement,
   for they had seen the Queen,
   stood in her presence as she passed briefly by.

Give me, Lord, a similar sense of wonder
   in the presence of Christ,
   an appreciation of the privilege I have,
   day after day,
   moment by moment,
   of knowing the one who is not just royalty
   but the King of kings and Lord of lords,
   greater than words can express
   or the mind comprehend.
Teach me to make time for him,
   not as an extra or afterthought
   but as my greatest joy and first priority,
   offering him my grateful praise and thankful service.
Amen.

73

The coins

It was innocent enough –
   just a handful of change,
   hardly enough to tempt anyone –
   but it set me thinking of other coins –
   thirty pieces of silver:
   enough to betray a closest friend
   and sell one's very soul.

My price may be higher, Lord,
   but I'm not as different as I like to think,
   money shaping my life in all kinds of ways,
   controlling my thoughts and influencing my decisions,
   holding me under its spell.
Forgive my foolish ways,
   for too often,
   without knowing it,
   I sell out to the highest bidder
   and betray you in turn.
Amen.

74

The glass of wine

'Red or white?' he asked,
    and after I'd made my choice, he poured it out,
    a glass of wine to accompany my meal
    and make a toast –
    one of life's little luxuries
    that I'd come to take for granted.

I recalled, Lord, another cup,
    another 'toast':
    Jesus serving his disciples with the words:
    'My blood,
    poured out for you and for many,
    for the forgiveness of sins.'
A cup not of pleasure but of pain,
    drunk not for himself but for others,
    representing the greatest of gifts,
    precious beyond words.
Whenever I drink, Lord,
    remind me of the true vine
    and the new wine you offer through it.
Amen.

75
The by-election defeat

He'd been a hero a week earlier,
   acclaimed and applauded wherever he went
   and certain, it seemed, of re-election,
   but, as the saying goes,
   a week is a long time in politics,
   scandal, tax rises and policy decisions taking their toll,
   until the anticipated victory evaporated
   into humiliating defeat.

You know all about fickle allegiance, Lord,
   mine all too often being found wanting
   when the chips are down.
Though I profess undying commitment,
   I'm like those who welcomed you into Jerusalem
   long ago,
   swift to look the other way
   when commitment proves costly:
   denying or abandoning you
   when service involves sacrifice.
Forgive the fragility of my faith,
   and give me an allegiance
   that stays true through thick and thin,
   just as you stay true to me.
Amen.

76
The pricked finger

It was nothing,
   just a tiny scratch
   where the nail had pricked my finger,
   but I sucked it ruefully,
   feeling sorry for myself
   if only for a moment.

But then, Lord, I remembered other nails,
   thrust deep into hands and feet,
   inflicting not just surface wounds
   but ripping through flesh and crushing bone,
   the pain too dreadful to contemplate,
   never mind the agony soon to follow.
For the immense love that could endure all this,
   willingly,
   gladly,
   for one such as me,
   receive my heartfelt praise.
Amen.

77

The hot cross buns

They're commonplace now,
    available in every supermarket
    on just about every day of the year,
    but I remember a time when things were different,
    the crosses placed there for Good Friday only –
    speaking of *another* cross,
    another day,
    a *special* day.

Though a reminder is lost, Lord,
    help me to see that a truth is gained:
    the cross of Christ,
    and the love of which it speaks,
    touching not merely a single day
    but *every* day,
    changing every moment and every*thing*.
Help me more fully to understand
    and celebrate your grace,
    so that it may shape my life,
    now
    and *always*.
Amen.

78
The broken vase

It was broken,
   shattered beyond repair,
   no way anyone could put it together again,
   however hard they might try.
The damage was too great
   and the pieces too small,
   the vase broken beyond redemption.

I forget, Lord, too easily, that your Son was also broken;
   that what he went through was no play-acting
   or sleight of hand,
   but suffering as real and terrible as I can imagine,
   endured until life was blotted out,
   seemingly ended for good.
Teach me to remember that truth,
   but to remember also that brokenness was not the end,
   for from death came life,
   from despair, hope
   and from sorrow, joy –
   your love bringing new beginnings.
And remind me, above all,
   that this same love is *still* at work,
   able to take broken people,
   broken lives,
   and make them whole.
Amen.

EASTER

79
The daffodils

They danced in the breeze,
    nodding their heads as if celebrating springtime –
    a blaze of colour where just months before
    all had been bare.
Once more the season had performed its magic,
    bringing new life out of old,
    new beginnings from what had seemed the end.

May the wonder of this season, Lord,
    point to a deeper wonder:
    your resurrection power
    that makes each day springtime,
    each moment a new dawn, full of promise.
Help me to recognise that, with you,
    every apparent ending leads to a fresh start,
    death itself the gate to life.
Amen.

80
The Easter eggs

They unwrapped them with excitement,
   eagerly breaking them apart
   to see what they held inside,
   such chocolate delights what this season, for them,
   was all about.

Speak deeper, Lord,
   offering through these eggs
   a reminder of birth and new life,
   your Son rising from the tomb.
Help me to greet this season with childlike enthusiasm,
   eager to celebrate what lies at its heart:
   your resurrection power and renewing love –
   what this season is *really* all about.
Amen.

81
The tall story

I didn't take him seriously,
    for he was clearly spinning a yarn,
    the claims so extravagant they were laughable,
    each more far-fetched than the next.
So I dismissed his words as so much nonsense,
    too fanciful to swallow.

It was the same centuries earlier:
    women rushing from the tomb,
    bubbling over with news of the resurrection,
    only for *their* words to be dismissed as nonsense,
    even by the disciples,
    the message seeming beyond belief,
    too good to be true.

Though I need to be sceptical sometimes, Lord,
    rather than believe everything I hear,
    save me from closing my mind too easily
    to what's beyond my experience.
Though I struggle at times with the idea of resurrection,
    so much causing me to question,
    remind me of the way you changed
    the lives of the apostles
    and of countless others since,
    transforming doubt to faith,
    sorrow to joy
    and fear to confidence.

Meet me, then, through the risen Christ,
   so that, incredible though it may seem,
   I may know him for myself,
   and share his life,
   now and for evermore.
Amen.

82
The bouncy ball

It bounced back again.
   time after time,
   the energy within it apparently inexhaustible,
   unable to be contained –
   and the harder it fell,
   so the higher it climbed,
   leaping up yet more spectacularly
   than it had done before.

Speak, Lord, of your resurrection power
   through which your Son rose again
   and his followers bounced back from despair.
Grant, then, the assurance that
   however low life may bring me
   and however hard I may fall,
   you will lift me up to new horizons,
   both now and for all eternity.
Amen.

83
The coffin

He was dead –
   there could be no denying it any longer,
   no more running from the truth.
The coffin before me spelt out the stark reality:
   that one I'd loved was gone,
   never to walk this earth again.

Remind me, Lord, that Jesus died,
   not just playing a part
   or going through the motions
   but enduring the darkness of death itself.
Yet remind me also that he rose again,
   greeting his disciples in the upper room,
   meeting them on the road,
   restoring faith, hope, joy and purpose.
So then, in the agony of bereavement,
   the trauma and despair of loss,
   assure me that beyond the grave lie new beginnings;
   that from dust and ashes you will bring new life,
   now and always.
Amen.

84
The newspaper exposé

They tried to suppress the truth,
    to hush it up with bribes and threats
    but they failed,
    for the reporter wouldn't let go,
    beavering away until she'd uncovered the facts
    and then printing the story for all to see.

I'm reminded, Lord, of another story,
    another time,
    but a similar attempt to suppress the truth
    and silence those who spoke it:
    the authorities bribing guards
    and intimidating believers
    in a bid to stifle news of the resurrection.

Remind me, Lord,
    that though truth may be threatened by falsehood,
    good by evil,
    love by hatred
    and life by death,
    your purpose will always come through,
    nothing finally allowed to frustrate
    your renewing power
    and redeeming grace.
Amen.

85

The school run

They waited to collect their children,
    standing outside the classroom or at the gates
    to meet them,
    none willing to risk their little one's safety
    by letting them walk home alone.
One day, perhaps,
    but as long as their kids were vulnerable,
    in need of support,
    they'd continue to be there for them –
    their welfare more important than anything.

Thank you, Lord, that you do not leave us alone,
    instead drawing alongside us through your Spirit.
Thank you that,
    just as you met with your followers on the road
    and your disciples in the upper room,
    so, in Christ, you meet with us on the journey of life,
    always there, in your resurrection power,
    to guide, protect, comfort and support,
    each of us valued as a little child,
    chosen and precious to you.
Amen.

86
The rabbits

There wasn't just one of them
    but hundreds,
    a whole warren at play,
    skipping across the dew-covered meadow,
    sniffing at the primroses and daffodils,
    and it seemed a perfect scene for the season,
    conjuring up images of Easter bunnies,
    spring flowers
    and a new dawn –
    altogether charming.

Thank you, Lord, for those images
    and the truth they point to,
    each speaking in their own way of new beginnings,
    a fresh start;
    but save me from sentimentalising this season,
    settling for cosy pictures
    and forgetting what it cost you to bring us life.
Remind me of how much you gave
    that I might receive,
    and help me to give something back in return,
    offering my love,
    my life,
    my all to you.
Amen.

87
The Easter bank holiday

They piled into their cars
   and headed for the motorway –
   this a weekend for going away,
   the first proper holiday of another year,
   or, if nothing else,
   a few days off,
   a break from the usual routine.

I value this holiday as much as anyone, Lord,
   and will enjoy it as much as I can,
   but remind me it is also a *holy* day,
   speaking of you and your love in Christ,
   his resurrection and the life you promise us in turn.
Wherever I am, then,
   and whatever I do,
   help me to remember
   what this season is ultimately about
   and to make space for *you* as well as for me.
Amen.

88
The solar eclipse

It was a strange moment,
    a once-in-a-lifetime experience –
    fascinating yet strangely eerie,
    the world for a moment going dark,
    shadow replacing sunshine,
    night usurping day.
But then it was over,
    the light returning once more,
    seemingly brighter than ever.

Remind me, Lord, when shadows darken my life
    and light seems suddenly extinguished,
    that you entered the darkness of death
    and rose victorious;
    that you experienced the full force of hatred
    and conquered it with love;
    that you took on the powers of evil
    and worked through them for good.
Remind me, then, that your light will always shine,
    nothing in heaven or earth finally able to overcome it.
Amen.

ASCENSION DAY

89
The view

I climbed the mountain
    and suddenly I could see what I'd never seen before,
    a panorama stretching out before me,
    giving a different perspective
    and a sense of wonder at the grandeur of it all.

Too easily, Lord,
    when it comes to faith,
    I settle for something less,
    my understanding of Christ limited,
    partial –
    the picture I have of him
    hidebound by my narrow preconceptions
    and finite comprehension.
Open my heart to the full extent of his greatness,
    the wonder of who he is and all he has done,
    so that I may recognise the one made flesh
    as the living Word;
    the one who humbled himself on the cross
    as the risen Saviour,
    who lives and reigns with you,
    one God,
    now and always.
Amen.

90
The honours list

They were suddenly elevated in the public eye,
    no longer simply Mr or Mrs,
    but Sir, Lord, MBE and the like –
    their names exalted,
    achievements recognised,
    contribution duly acknowledged.
And why not? –
    for they deserved acclaim,
    each having excelled in their own way.

Whatever I call you, Lord,
    however much I honour your name,
    it can never be enough,
    never even begin to express the homage you are due
    for you are higher than my highest thoughts,
    greater than the human mind can ever comprehend,
    worthy of all praise and adoration.
Help me, today and always,
    to worship you as you deserve.
Amen.

PENTECOST

91
The wind farm

They turned in harmony,
   the mighty sails catching the wind
   and harnessing its power –
   enough to meet the needs of a small town,
   year in, year out,
   providing energy for all.

Energise my life, Lord, by the breath of your Spirit,
   giving power for living
   through your love and goodness.
Open my heart to your presence flowing within,
   blowing away whatever keeps me from you,
   so that I may live and work more faithfully
   for your kingdom,
   this and every day.
Amen.

92
The iron smelting

It went into the furnace as nuggets of ore,
   rough and ready,
   but came out as liquid metal,
   pure and unalloyed,
   ready to be moulded and fashioned
   after being refined by fire.

Refine me, Lord, through the flame of your Spirit,
   cleansing, purifying and recasting my life.
Come now with tongues of redeeming fire
   and create from what I am
   something new for you.
Amen.

TRINITY SUNDAY

93
The 3-D glasses

They made such a difference,
  giving me a sense of being there,
  involved in the action –
  for they opened up new dimensions,
  giving a fresh perspective on all,
  what I'd known before in theory
  suddenly experienced in practice.

Help me to see *you* like that, Lord:
  in all your glory
  rather than the single dimension
  I all too easily reduce you to.
Help me to glimpse you as Father –
  providing,
  guiding,
  caring for me each day;
  to see you as Son –
  sharing my humanity
  and walking this earth;
  to experience you as Spirit –
  alive within,
  prompting, comforting,
  teaching and equipping.
Give me a fuller picture of who and what you are,
  and an awareness that no dimension or measure
  can finally contain the wonder of it all.
Amen.

94
The relations

One called me 'son',
   another 'dad',
   another 'brother',
   each of them seeing me in a different light,
   but of course I was the same person,
   the relationship shaping the perception.

I can't push the comparison, Lord,
   for somehow you're *both* three persons yet one,
   but it offers a clue, nonetheless,
   for I *too* relate to you in different ways:
   as Father, Son and Holy Spirit;
   Creator, Redeemer and Counsellor,
   a God above, alongside yet within me,
   wonderful beyond words.
Though that doesn't explain away the mystery,
   may it constantly remind me that knowing you
   involves a personal encounter
   and living experience,
   touching every part of who and what I am
   each and every day.
Amen.

FATHER'S DAY

95

The Father's Day card

It didn't say much –
    simply 'Daddy, I love you',
    the words scrawled spider-like across the page –
    yet it said everything,
    the card bringing tears to my eyes:
    every letter and squiggle,
    blot and correction,
    reinforced the look in her eyes
    as she proudly handed it across
    with a transparent devotion
    that said more than words could begin to.

Help me, Lord, to show my love for *you*,
    not through sophisticated language
    or polished prayers
    but through true commitment,
    responding with childlike trust, gratitude
    and affection
    to your fatherly care.
Teach me to open my heart to you,
    as you have so freely done to me.
Amen.

HARVEST
THANKSGIVING

96
The good and bad harvests

It was a bumper crop,
    the best ever,
    and why not? –
    for from sowing to reaping
    it had been carefully tended,
    the latest technology used throughout
    to secure a maximum yield,
    increased productivity.

It was a poor crop,
    the worst ever,
    all the effort that had gone into it
    thwarted by prolonged drought
    followed by heavy storms,
    the seasons out of kilter,
    nature's delicate balance undermined.

Teach me, Lord, that the skills and ingenuity
    you have given humankind
    can either sustain your creation or destroy it.
Remind me that the fate of the planet is in our hands,
    each having a part to play.
Help me to do my bit faithfully,
    and grant that others may do the same.
Amen.

97
The fruit bowl

It was a mouth-watering selection,
    the bowl stacked with a host of fruits
    all carefully nurtured until ready for harvest –
    enough there not just for me but the whole family,
    bringing pleasure and health to us all.

What harvest do *I* produce, Lord, if any at all?
What fruits can be seen in my life,
    testifying to the work of your Spirit,
    your presence within?
I speak of love, joy, peace and gentleness –
    these to name but some –
    but so often the facts deny the theory,
    such fruits conspicuously lacking.
Reach out in mercy,
    and nurture the seeds you have sown within me,
    so that they may truly grow and flourish,
    to your glory.
Amen.

ALL SAINTS' DAY

98
The teacher

She explained what to do,
   again and again,
   but it was no good,
   I couldn't grasp it,
   couldn't for the life of me take in what she was saying.
So, finally, she *showed* me,
   going through the process step by step –
   an example for me to follow.

Remind me, Lord, of the great company of your people
   who have gone before me,
   famed or forgotten,
   celebrated or overlooked –
   all who have run their race and kept the faith,
   walking the way of Christ to their journey's end.
Help me to learn from them,
   so that one day I too may give a lead,
   inspiring others to love and serve you in turn.
Amen.

99

The rare breeds park

They were a joy to behold,
    an array of animals once common, now rare,
    brought together in a working farm –
    each a prize specimen,
    a classic of its kind.

Inspire me, Lord, through rare breeds of another sort –
    those whose lives point to Christ;
    their thoughts, words and deeds
    speaking in unison of him,
    their commitment unmistakable,
    faith sure
    and love evident:
    an inspiration to generations since.
Help me to follow in their footsteps
    so that, despite my many faults,
    I may in some way rank among their number.
Amen.

REMEMBRANCE DAY

100
The war memorial

It was a sorry sight
   despite the poppies laid around it,
   for the years had taken their toll,
   moss and lichen covering the stonework
   and the plaque tarnished,
   green now with age.
Yet it represented a sight sorrier still:
   fields strewn with bodies,
   young men cut down in their prime,
   unimaginable suffering and slaughter –
   those who, unlike the memorial,
   did not grow old.

Remind me, Lord,
   lest I forget,
   of the debt I owe –
   the life made possible through the death of others.
Help me to cherish and nurture the things they died for –
   liberty,
   justice
   and peace –
   so that their sacrifice will not have been in vain.
Amen.